Here Comes the Sun

arranged for lever or pedal harp by Sylvia Woods

words and music by George Harrison

This sheet music includes three solo harp arrangements.

Page 1 - for lever harps tuned to the key of C

Page 5 - for lever harps tuned to flats

Page 9 - for pedal harp

A note for lever harp players

There is another possible fingering for the left hand "1-2-3-4" in measures 14 to 15. These notes could all be played with the left thumb in a "flat hand muffle" position. Information on how to do this technique can be found at www.harpcenter.com/muffle

This phrase is also found in measures 29-30, 63-64, and 66-67. All of these passages are notated with a flat hand muffle (+) in the pedal harp version.

1

Here Comes the Sun
for lever harps tuned to the key of C

Words and Music by GEORGE HARRISON
Harp arrangement by SYLVIA WOODS

Set your sharping levers for the key signature, and then re-set the levers shown above.
Sharping lever changes are indicated with diamond notes and also with octave wording.
Many lever changes are very quick and need to be made exactly on the beats indicated.

Moderately

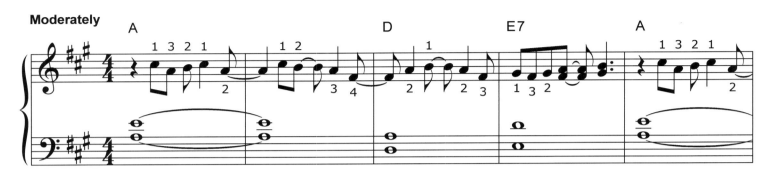

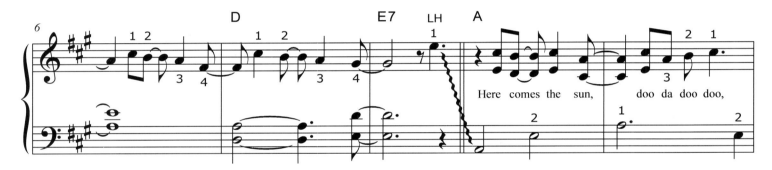

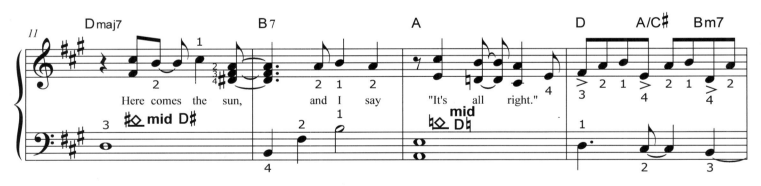

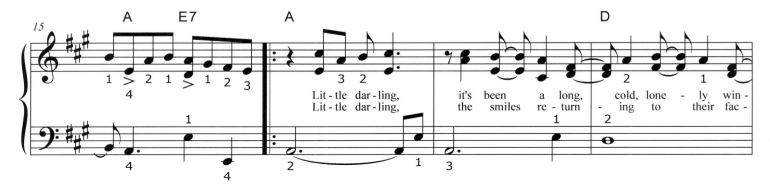

3

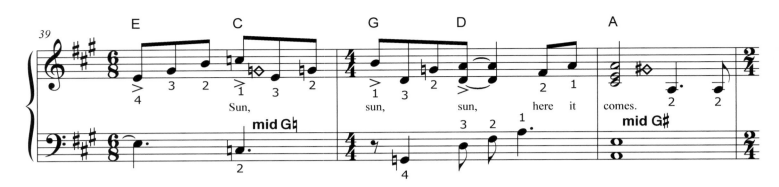

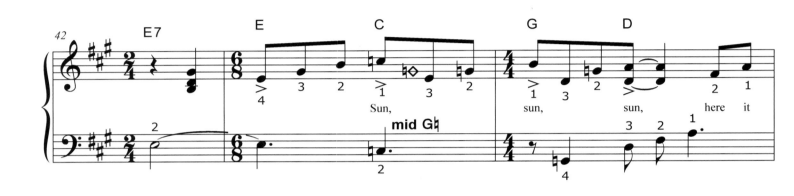

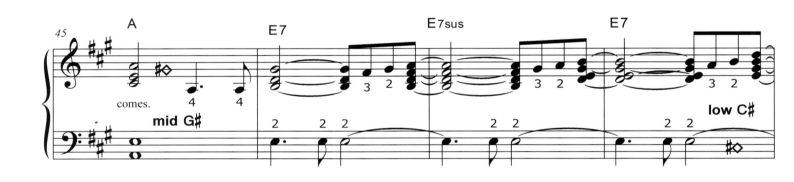

Here Comes the Sun

for lever harps tuned to flats

Words and Music by GEORGE HARRISON
Harp arrangement by SYLVIA WOODS

Set your sharping levers for the key signature, and then re-set the levers shown above.
Sharping lever changes are indicated with diamond notes and also with octave wording.
Many lever changes are very quick and need to be made exactly on the beats indicated.

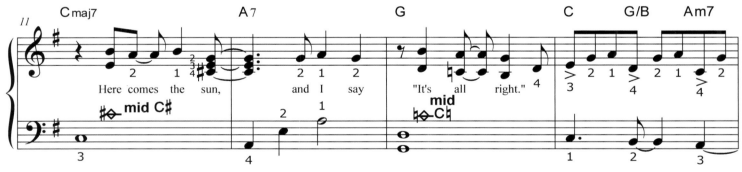

very low Bb

mid Bb

mid F♮

mid F#

Play with RH
for page turn

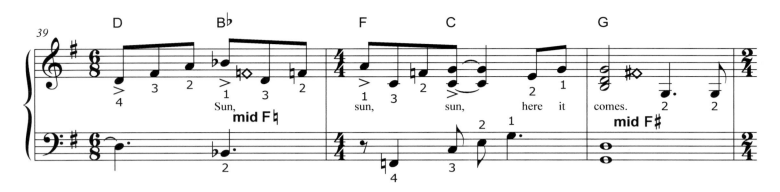

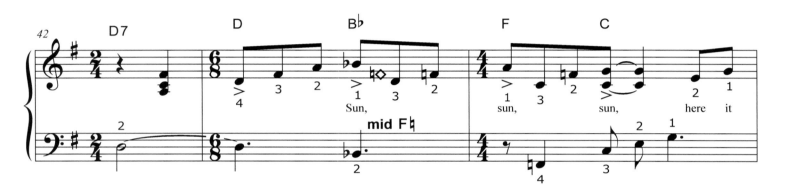

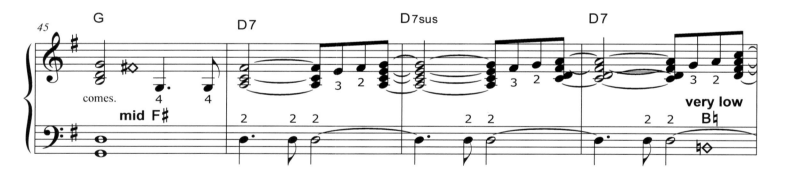

9

Here Comes the Sun
for pedal harps

Words and Music by GEORGE HARRISON
Harp arrangement by SYLVIA WOODS

Moderately

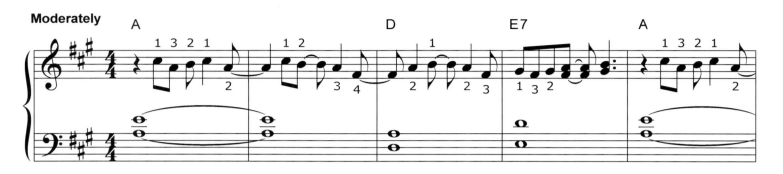

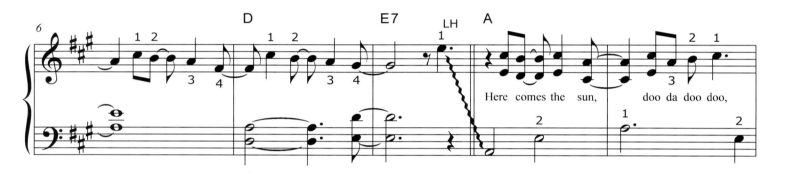

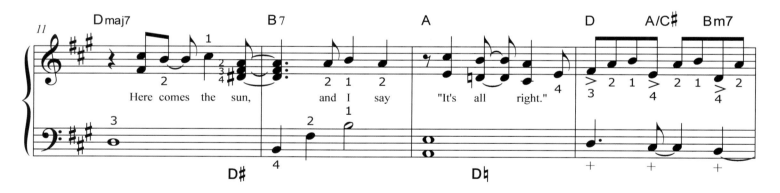

More Pop Music Arrangements for Harp by Sylvia Woods

While My Guitar Gently Weeps
by George Harrison

Lennon & McCartney for the harp book

A Thousand Years
Bring Him Home
Castle on a Cloud
A Charlie Brown Christmas
Dead Poets Society
Everything
Fields of Gold
Fireflies
Game of Thrones
Hallelujah

Happy
House at Pooh Corner
Into the West
It's a Beautiful Day
La La Land selections
Marry Me
My Heart Will Go On
Over the Rainbow
Perfect
Photograph
River Flows in You
Safe & Sound
Say Something
Stairway to Heaven
Stay with Me
Unchained Melody
Unforgettable

DISNEY & PIXAR MUSIC
76 Disney Songs book
Beauty and the Beast
Brave
Frozen
How Does a Moment Last Forever
Lava
Tangled
Theme from Up

OTHER BOOKS
Favorites from the 50s
Groovy Songs of the 60s
John Denver Love Songs
22 Romantic Songs
Andrew Lloyd Webber
The Wizard of Oz

Available from harp music retailers and www.harpcenter.com

Thanks
I'd like to thank Paul Baker, Anne Roos, and Denise Grupp-Verbon for their invaluable help

© 2018 by Sylvia Woods
Woods Music & Books
Sylvia Woods Harp Center
PO Box 223434, Princeville HI 96722
www.harpcenter.com

U.S. $8.99

HL00291398

ISBN 978-0-936661-86-5

HAL•LEONARD®
7777 W. BLUEMOUND RD. P.O. BOX 13819
MILWAUKEE, WISCONSIN 53213

More Pop Harp Music
by Sylvia Woods

All of Me
Beauty and the Beast
Music from Disney-Pixar's Brave
Bring Him Home from Les Misérables
Castle on a Cloud from Les Misérables
A Charlie Brown Christmas
Dead Poets Society
Everything
John Denver Love Songs
76 Disney Songs
Fields of Gold
Fireflies
Music from Disney Frozen
Groovy Songs of the 60s
Four Holiday Favorites
Hallelujah
Happy

House at Pooh Corner
Into the West from The Lord of the Rings
It's a Beautiful Day
Lennon and McCartney
Marry Me
My Heart Will Go On from Titanic
Over the Rainbow from The Wizard of Oz
River Flows in You
22 Romantic Songs
Safe & Sound
Say Something
Music from Disney Tangled
A Thousand Years
Andrew Lloyd Webber Music
The Wizard of Oz
Theme from Disney-Pixar's Up

Available from harp music retailers and www.harpcenter.com

U.S. $8.99

HL00121104

Exclusively Distributed By

Hal•Leonard
CORPORATION
7777 W. BLUEMOUND RD. P.O. BOX 13819
MILWAUKEE, WISCONSIN 53213

ISBN 978-0-936661-46-9

9 780936 661469

8